PRAYER IN POETRY FOR THE CHRISTIAN MOTHER

VICKY SPYROU-ANDRIOTIS
PRAYER IN POETRY
FOR THE
CHRISTIAN MOTHER

PUBLISHED BY
VICKY SPYROU-ANDRIOTIS
CONNECTICUT, USA

Published 2008 by Vicky Spyrou-Andriotis

Printed and bound in the
United States of America
ISBN-10: 0-9821808-0-2
ISBN-13: 978-0-9821808-0-8

Prayer In Poetry For The Christian Mother
www.vickyandriotis.com

Cover and Book Design – Vicky Spyrou-Andriotis

Dedicated To Him, for He inspires and
guides me always.

Written for Manny, from Mother to Son, so
that I might inspire and guide him.

Contents

"And whatever things you ask in prayer, believing, you will receive."

Matthew 21:22 NKJV™

LITTLE BIRD

Little Mother
Find strength
And let your little bird fly
Have faith
That he will soar
And not falter
For he is guided by the whisper in the breeze

Little Mother
Teach him to pray to our Heavenly Father
That he may be favored
And his life may be blessed

Let your mind be eased by the knowledge
that with guidance from above
He will do
As he has been taught
And so
Let your little bird
Fly

TAKE A MOMENT

Be gentle
Be kind
Do not allow the cares of the day
To influence your words
To those you love

A moment of reflection
A moment of prayer
To find your true self
Can sweeten a bitter word
Can bring a smile to one's lips
Instead of a tear to one's eyes

Leave your anger behind
Let your love be your guide
And you will find that when you speak
Your words will be music to the ears

We Are

We are patience
Not always in abundance
But as often as possible

We are love
Unconditional
Infinite and boundless

We are wisdom
Though forever in pursuit of

We are "Mother"

It is the weight of the world
It is endless joy
It is by the grace of God
That we are
"Mother"

Through joy and through pain
For better or for worse
There is no one we'd rather be

We are now
And always
"Mother"

BEAUTY

So much beauty in this world
I am blinded
Such detail
Such thoughtfulness in its creation

And how blessed am I
For that which is most beautiful of all
Lays his head upon my shoulder
And finds warmth
And comfort
In my embrace

Though all creation fills my eyes
And I am surrounded by more beauty in
each day
Than I can even comprehend

I give thanks and praise
For I have found and understand
That which is most beautiful
And precious
Of all

THE SOUND OF YOU

I sat and listened to my heart today
Lord
What I heard was You

My heart
So full of love
So full of joy
Both impossible without Your touch
Without Your existence

For without You
Our days would be dark
Our time empty
There could be no tomorrow

I pray that those I cherish
Those I love
Live their lives with their hearts full of You
Overflowing with love and joy
Knowing better todays
And brighter tomorrows

And when they listen to their hearts
May they always hear
The sound of You

FOR GRANTED

Make no mistake
Every morning that your eyes open
Is a miracle
Every time that you feel loved
Or that you love another
Is a miracle

Open your eyes and do not take these things
for granted
See them for what they are

Sometimes it is difficult for you to embrace
the sunrise
Or love
Or the beauty that's around you
But without these things
Our lives are nothing more than empty,
meaningless moments
Tumbling by

Take the time to LIVE
Take the time to see and feel and taste the
things, the people, that fill your world
That fill your nights
That fill your days

Take a little piece of life
And hold it
Don't let go
Hear the music on a wind and listen
Before it's gone

Climb the height of a mountain
Swim the depth of a sea
Run the length of the horizon
Let your mind fly among shapeless clouds
Search for the buried treasure within you
Take each thing as a miracle

But do not take these things for granted

WHEN I PRAY

And when a mother prays
She looks to the needs of her children
Considers the needs of her husband
Envisions the needs of those dear

And when a mother prays
It is for the benefit of those she loves
Those she knows
And those she doesn't
For the world around her

A mother's prayers come
From deep within her heart
Bottomless
Unlimited
Open
Selfless

And for this
She is loved
And tended to

WHAT I AM

I am woman
I am mother
I am God made
And Heaven sent
Like all mothers before me
And all those to come

Guardians and teachers
Of His most beloved creations
Our children
To whom the Kingdom of Heaven belongs
Whose innocence
And faith
Belief and love
Shall be nurtured
And preserved

I pray for the strength
To keep them from sin
My purpose is clear
And with faith and love
I shall fulfill it

Amen

BEHOLD

Oh!
How blessed I am
To behold
That which
I had only dreamed of
And prayed for

To hold you in my arms
For the first time
And forever
God smiled upon me
At that moment
Through your gaze

So radiant
Unbelievable
Unforgettable
And undeniably
A God-given moment
To last
A lifetime

QUIET YOUR MIND

Stop!
Your mind, it dances in circles
But you seek
To quiet
The music
For now
And find the rhythm in the dance

Complex
And difficult at times
The steps elude you
For you are not trying to understand

So simple the rules
And help is there for the asking
And believing, it shall be given
To those who join the dance

Allow yourself to be lead
And step
By step
You will feel the rhythm of life's dance
Inside yourself
Through Him

IN YOUR TIME

Infinitesimal
The time we have
The lives we lead

Let your time
Bring about change
Let it be
In service to others
In service to God
For with Him is where you will spend
eternity

Bring Light
To places that only know darkness
To those who have little
Give what you can
Believe that you matter
Believe that change is in your hands
And you will leave a mark
That will open
The Gates
To you

SISTERS

My sisters
Teach what you know
Love each other
Draw strength from one another
Let your thoughts be quiet
And your words be kind
And do as He would have you do

Bitterness and envy have no place among
you
For you are the only ones who can truly
understand each others hearts
Each others joys
And fears

Be welcoming and sincere
Do not speak or do in secret what your
children would find shameful in public

Your are strong and wise
You are as good as He made you
And as your children see you
You are all sisters in your commonality
In your goals
In your dreams
And in this life
And in the next

LABOR OF LOVE

Reward enough
This life we lead
Ours is a labor of love
One that is full of precious moments
And memories in the making

Reward enough
To see the fruits of our labor
In the actions of those
Whom we teach

We plant
Inside their minds and hearts
The seeds that grow to be kindness
And love
Strength
And courage
Charity and patience

And we watch these virtues grow
Into the products
Of our labor
Of love

AS IT SHOULD BE

When the evening comes
And the day
Feels like
Every other
I look to the things that matter
And I pray for another day

When the sun
Rises in the sky
And our gifts from God still surround me
I understand
That life is as it should be

And when the occupants of life seem weary
And tired
When they are swept by the urge
To run away
I hope they pause
I hope they pray
I hope they listen for the sound of those who
they love
And understand
Their life
And significance
And thank God
For another day

FAMILY

Through marriage
Through God
Family grows
Through a union
Through a bond
With him whom you have chosen
Come those who watched him grow

Through understanding and love
Through patience and
Respect
New bonds can be formed

Delicately
Gently
Tend to them
So that these bonds grow
And are never broken

Where there are misunderstandings
Seek guidance and pray
For the capacity to see clearly
The ability to speak gently
And the desire
To forgive

THE EYES OF A CHILD

I marvel
At his simplicity
His joys are many
His needs are few
To see through the eyes of a child
Such a blessing
So rare
But don't think it impossible
Attained through prayer
Ask to see the world as it was intended
Leave your heart open
To its pleasures
Its joys

Approach each thing
With a sense of wonder
And know that something new
Can be learned every day

And when this prayer is answered
You will see
Through the eyes
Of a child

BY ONE NAME

How do I honor you
For the sacrifices you've made
The courage you've shown
For your affection
For your love

How do I make clear
My gratitude
For the needs that you filled
The values you instilled
The dreams you encouraged
And the roads that you paved to ease my
journey

There is but one way to honor you most
To show you my love
To thank God for your presence
And impact
And influence in my life
And that is to call you
By one name alone

"Mother"

TO UNDERSTAND

Lord
For this I pray
To see
As he sees
To feel
As he feels
So that I might know
From where his thoughts
And actions arise

Empathy
Compassion
Both essential
To our connection

They will strengthen our bond
And our appreciation
For one another

Make our tongues incapable of
forming
Acrid
Bitter words

Let us understand each other instead

Amen

GATHER TOGETHER

Children
Of God
Gather together
Mothers, Fathers
Sons and Daughters

Make known from where you gather your
strength
Let us bring God's family
Together
Where it belongs
And shall remain

We are Children of God!
We who love and are loved
Who try to evict hate from our hearts
And our lives

Pray together
Be together
Come together as a family
For we are all
Children of God

I SENSED YOU

I sensed You today
When I felt a bit afraid
I sensed You today
When I wondered about life
I sensed You today
When I worried for my child
I sensed You today
When I sought a hand to hold

I feel You now
As I read these words
I feel You now
As I seek inspiration
I feel You now
As I take a step forward
I feel You
As I realize
That it won't be as hard as I thought
As long as I can sense
You

GENTLE MOTHER

O Lord
I ask forgiveness
When patience eludes me
And anger takes its place
I ask that You show me
Lead me
Help me
To be a loving example
A gentler mother
That I see in his mistakes
The opportunity to teach
Instead of chastise

Help me to stand firm
But without anger

Help me to find the words to speak
And let "he who has ears"[1] hear
So that he may always
Be worthy enough
To call himself
A child of God

---

[1] The Holy Bible (NKJV) - Matthew 13:9

SACRIFICE

Lord
If I should suffer anxiety
And worry
For the sake of our children
And watch them grow
To be glad and kind
Prosperous and wise
I shall be elated
And rejoice
And feel justified

Should I require to sacrifice
Of myself
So that they may thrive
And bring glory to You
And peace to my soul
And that I might see my sacrifice
Have purpose and reason
Then I shall sacrifice gladly
And without hesitation
And I will thank You
For the reasons
To have sacrificed

Amen

YOUR CHOICES

In the eyes of she who raised you
In the heart of the one you call mother
Know that you are
The one
And the only

The one for whom her life revolves
The one whom she would give it for
Easily
Freely
Lovingly

And when you are choosing your actions
Or considering your deeds
Or searching for the right words to speak
Think first of God
Then her
And know that you have chosen
Admirably

MARY AND ELIZABETH

Oh Mothers
Of Great Sons
Oh Mary and Elizabeth
Grant us your wisdom
Your courage
An ounce of your strength

Help us to find the answers, that we may
know them instinctively
Make clear to us the mysteries of
motherhood
The knowledge of them inherent

So that we may follow in the footsteps of
your greatness
For You are Blessed
And with admiration and love
We pray
That we may attain but a fragment
Of your abilities
As mothers

DAUGHTER

Daughter, I have been
Therefore listen
Without pride
And tuck your arrogance away
While I impart what I know is true

Satisfaction can not be obtained by
bickering and disputes
Trust in your mother's love, and that she
thinks only of you, even when her words
might anger you

Trust your intuition
But know that a true mother's advice is
given only with the benefit of her child in
mind
It is selfless and never hurtful, never unkind

Do not suppose that your solutions or
opinions are best
Listen to the sound of her experience, and
you may find that some are better
Above all, be certain that your words to her
Or about her
Are spoken with love
And respect

First

What a miracle
This first day
What joy, this first step
What laughter, these first words
Such hope, starting school

What pride, this first win
What excitement, this first love

With faith, we watch
Through prayer, we achieve
The "firsts" of our lives
Fleeting
Momentary
But forever
And deeply
Ingrained into our hearts
And our thoughts
And we are forever
And deeply
Grateful

TO BE

To be worthy of my child's love
My husband's admiration
My mother's pride
And God's blessings
I endeavor

To be considered kind
And wise
Humble
Yet strong
That my children seek my guidance
I pray

To lead a life of worth
One pleasing to Him
One who inspires and helps
Those who seek
I pray

NEARER TO YOU

It is not for the promise of reward that I pray
It is to be nearer to You
And though my prayers
Are where others can see
They are free of vanity
There is no arrogance
There is no pride
Only the desire to lead those in my charge
In prayer
To remind them
To teach them
To inspire them
To speak to You
As I do
To give them the words to speak
To help them to pray
To help others be
Closer to You

DRY YOUR EYES

Dry your eyes
Winter comes quickly
Rain upon the windowsill
Will wash your fears away

Another storm brews
Thunder rages
Lightning in its glory
Hold tight to those you hold dear
And this storm
Will not get the best of you

Your faith
Your love
Will keep you safe
When the storms of life
Draw near
Be mindful of what's important
And precious
And in time
The storms will pass you by

REASONS TO STAY

Do not wander through
Months of tomorrows
Carelessly
Purposeless
Sorrowful

Do not leave
Thinking the place is the cause
Of your distress
For that comes from within
And can not be avoided

But if you wish to keep your heart alive
To fill it with hope
And immeasurable joy
Look into the eyes of a child
The smile of a friend
And God above
And there
You will find
The reasons to stay

LOVE FINDS YOU

Do you question why there is love?
Do not
Instead, accept it
Cherish it
And do not wonder how it found its way to
you
For if you give it freely
He bestows it upon you
Through the birth of a child
Through the bond of marriage
Through the presence of a friend

And I pray
That love will always find you
And that you send it back
Out into the world
So that it may be stored
And cherished
In the hearts of all
You know

THIS LIFE

This life
Is not meant to be lived in anger
And God
Did not create us so that we may live alone
This life
Is meant to show you
His world
His way
From where you came
And where you belong

You can not live this life a stranger
For you are His beloved
Loved by Him who knows you well and best
of all
And by those whom He has placed in your
path
With whom you've united
Bonded
And call your very own

YOU

You inhabit my then
You inhabit my now
All would be uncertain
Fruitless
Without Your impact
Without this awareness
Of You

I do not dwell on who I used to be
I am only grateful
For the woman that I've become
Through You
Your word
And the thought of You
Have nurtured my soul
And body
And enabled me
Empowered me
Inspired me
To be
Who I am meant
To be

DELIGHT

What brings delight
To a mother's life?
The contentment of her child
For her child is the
"Apple of her eye"
The source of her worries
The source of her joys
The axis
On which her world revolves

Her duty
Her life's work
A test of her fortitude
And yet
She never wonders
From where her strength
And her endurance
Are derived
For she knows she only has
To look towards Heaven
And ask in prayer
And to her
It is granted

HOME

It is only with love
That this house
Is made a home

It is only with God
That we know this love

These walls do not stand alone
Independently
They are held together
By the family whom they shelter
Without whom
These walls contain
But an empty, hollow space

Now they are filled with laughter
Gladness
And God
May that be
As it is
Forever more

GIVE MORE

Woman
Tired and weary
Imagines she's offered
All she can
Looks again
At the needs of the world
And gives some more

She does not wait
To be asked
Does not expect
To be told

She does not hesitate
Her heart knows no restrictions
Her door is opened wide
As she sees the opportunity
The chance
Walk through it
To give some more

And for the opportunity
And the ability
She thanks the Lord

TIME

Time
A friend
Given to us, by the Grace of God
A place to begin
A place to end
An invisible boundary
By which we plan our days
Our years
Our future
With which we remember our past
Within which we live our present
All
Is a matter of time

Wisdom
Knowledge
Faith
Love and happiness
Are acquired
And grow
All
In a matter of time

THIS SOUND

O Lord, what is this sound that fills me
And plays upon my heartstrings
Triggering sweet memories of my youth
Images of faces, now unseen
Seeing them as clearly as the moment I
inhabit now
What is this sound carried through the air,
enveloping me
Emotions I'd forgotten, now lingering
Hovering
Suspended before me, I can almost touch
them
What is this joyous sound that brings these
memories tumbling forward?

Ah
But it is sweet music , sweet hymns of praise
One of the most magnificent of all the
abilities you've blessed us with , that is to
create it
And as thanks
We use it
To sing sweet hymns of praise to You

ENDEAVOR

God in Heaven
Holy Spirit that surrounds me
Grant me success
In my endeavor to be
A mother worthy to be called one
Bless me with the gift of words
So that I may speak wisely
So that the right words
Never escape me

Grant that I recognize which battles to fight
And which to let fade away

That I may always be clear-sighted
That I am good
And honorable
And know my place
In this life
And that I always have a place
In my child's
I pray

THIS STRUGGLE

Do not feel that your life's a struggle
Rejoice in what you have
And understand
That God knows your needs
As well as your burdens

You must believe
That God will provide
That He knows your fears
And your sorrows
Your aspirations
Your dreams

Believe that there are blessings
Meant for you
Believe
With all you have
And all that you are
Believe
And changes
Will
Come

FOUND MY PLACE

I seek my place
In Your house
Lord
For there I know
I will be cared for
As I care for
All
Who enter mine
Friends and strangers alike
Stand side by side
And I am at peace
With You in our midst

And I feel the power of our faith
And I feel the power of our prayers
And I know that I have found my place
In the house
Of
Our Lord

MOTHERHOOD

In a moment
Quietly, like a whisper
Comes the circumstance
Action
Word
That wakes up your very soul
Sends tremors
Through your very existence
Sends you hurling into an
Opposite direction

Perhaps it leaves you hopeful
Perhaps it gives you strength
Perhaps it renews your faith
Whichever is accomplished
It will shake your foundation
The thought
The idea
The reality
Of Motherhood
Leaves you forever changed

PROUDLY, MY CHILD

Proudly
I say
You are my child
Confident and hopeful
Mighty and brave
You lift my spirits
My heart, it soars

Your courage is evident
Your compassion overflows
I pray you use
The things you are
To better the lives of all
Whom you encounter

To lift them up
To affect change

Praise and thank Him
Every day
By giving of yourself
What the Lord has given you
And know
That you are blessed

SUPPLY OF LOVE

To us
The fortunate
The caregivers
God has provided
An infinite supply of love

It expands
It grows
It is ageless
Eternal
It will outlast
The sky above
And the earth itself
It will never wane
It will never falter
Our capacity to love
Can not be measured

It is powerful
Profound
And can only be understood
By a mother
And her child

SOME DAY

Some day
I will tell you
How I rocked you to sleep
In my warm embrace
When your tears wouldn't cease
I prayed for strength

Some day
You will hear
How I lay by your bed
As you slept, trembling, and ill
While I prayed for your health

Some day
You will know
How I've given my heart
Instantly
Willingly
Completely
And I pray that when you do
You'll be proud
To be my son

I COMMIT MYSELF

I commit myself to you Lord
And to all You have taught us through Your
words, and through Your deeds

Through your example and sacrifice
I will be
A woman who leads her family with her
faith
With what she knows to be true
With her passionate belief and trust
And hope
In all that is good and all that is true
And all that
Comes
From
You

SINCERE

For a life that is sincere
In all that I am
Or become
Or do
That I am known for the sincerity in my
emotions
My sentiments
My beliefs
So that when I speak
My children are confident
That I believe in
What I say
And say
What I believe
And on this they can depend

May God grant me
What I seek
This I pray

Amen

YOUR WORDS

My child
Do not let words of envy
Or jealousy
Spill from your lips
Gossip is unbecoming
More to the person who speaks it
Than to the person of whom you speak
Whether it is an enemy
Or worse
A friend

Let only words of kindness fill your mouth
And your heart
Otherwise
None at all

Remember what I've taught you
And consider whether what you do
Would be pleasing or not
To Him
For it is He
Who will hold you accountable
And ultimately
Who you will answer to
And so, be sure of the kindness in your heart
For He can not be fooled

I REMEMBER

I remember, Lord
Even with distractions
And all the noise in my head
It is You, Lord
Who I remember first

To You I turn
To You I pray
It is You who comforts me
And You who I depend on

You assuage my fears
Only through You do I find courage
I pray to You
And know the outcome will have purpose
I pray to You
Knowing, and believing
That my prayers
Will be heard
And answered

PRAISE GOD

What gratitude can one express
When angels have interceded
Have made themselves known
By otherwise inexplicable occurrences
That can only be possible
Through their intervention

There is nothing to be said
Or enough that can be done
To show the gratitude a mother has
As she watches her family
Peacefully
Contently
Gathered together
After a calamity, averted

She gladly falls to her knees
Humbly
Praying
Giving praise to God
And knowing
There's so much more
To be done
In gratitude

MY HEART FOLLOWS

Child of God
Child of mine
You are love
Personified
You are like the blood
That flows through my veins
You give me life
You warm me down to my very soul

I see you
I watch you
And understand
That life has meaning
And that we are forever
Connected
To each other
And our lives
Are intertwined
And held together
By many threads
And so
That no matter where you are
My heart
Follows you there

YOUR DAUGHTER

Father
I see your love
I witness it
From Father to daughter
For one and all
We are your children

From this bounty
That is my life
I know your gifts
Firsthand
For I live them
Daily

And I offer my thanks
For all that is
And all that I have
And all that will be

Amen

LIONESS

Sisters in motherhood
The Lord has made us
With the ferocity
And the bravery
Of a lioness
Protecting
And caring
For her young
The same as we

Graced with the ability to provide
And nurture
Even when circumstance
Tests our determination
We persist
Insist
That the needs of our young
Are filled
Before all others

Powerful and
Valiant
We are as the lioness

THE HEART BELIEVES

Silently moving
Toward a blue day
Through clouds
A burst of sun
Gray days behind me

For I prayed for the warmth of Your sunlight
And though petals are frozen
Middle of winter
You offer a warm breeze
Which flows through me

My eyes can not see
What the heart believes
Prayers
Take me far
From the place I am standing
To a place of hope
And peace
Away from this cold day
And closer
To the sunlight

Words I Say

Have mercy, Lord
Do not leave me to wonder
If my answers are unwise
Their impact is certain
And they must be correct
As they might change a life

When a son strays
When he has been unkind
A mother should know
The words to say
To change the direction
Of his life

Lord, supply the words
Let them pour from my lips
And fill his ears
Fill his heart
That he will seek to change his ways
And live in a way
That brings him closer to You

SHE IS

She is her own woman
For the Lord has made her so
She will flourish
Thrive
For inside
She is brimming with hope
She is sustained by her faith
And propelled by her faith

She loves
She is loved
She inspires
And is inspired
She teaches

She possesses a quiet, inner strength
That is
Incomparable
For it is God given and safeguarded by Him

And so are her qualities
That she might serve
Her purpose
And His will, be done

THERE I AM

Look behind you
There I Am
All around you
There I Am
Close your eyes
There I Am
Why do you seem surprised?

I'm your shadow
There I Am
Right beside you
There I Am
I heard you calling
Here I Am
Your faith has brought Me near

Where shadows find you
Where the moon lights your way
Do not fear the darkness
For there
I'll
Be

LIVING WORD

Flowing
With eloquence
Softly
Heard with my heart
It spreads through me
It is
Like wildfire
Through my veins
Spreading
The living word
With every beat
Of my heart
Further
Deeper
It ebbs
And flows
Ebbs
And flows
Then spills
Out into the world
As it is
Meant to be

BECAUSE OF HER

It is written
She must be honored
And her worth can not be measured
For she is noble
And God-fearing
And from husband and child
She must receive praise

It is of her doing
And by her hands
That her house is a home
And that wisdom and love
Are plentiful within it

It is because of her
That their hearts have been opened to God
Through her they've been enlightened
And for this
Husband and child
Shall offer praise
And appreciation
For they've been
Blessed
With her presence
In their lives

WHAT THE LORD HAS DONE

What the Lord has done for you
Impossible to grasp
Receive your blessings
Your children
Your loved ones
And rejoice
Be light
And express your gratitude
With generosity
Toward others
Hold a hand
That needs comforting
Speak a kind word
To someone who is suffering
Give what is needed
For the body
And the soul
For you are exceedingly blessed
And so
Let your gratitude be felt
By all

SAFE

Lord
I fear for him
I beseech you
Send a guardian to watch over him
To protect him

Let not the errors of my past
Affect his future
Keep him safe
From any who wish to do him harm

Teach him when to stand his ground
And when to walk away

May his words be enough
To quell
Anger in others
And bring peace
Instead

Amen

FRIENDSHIP

Our spirits
Kindred
Together we have grown
Our friendship
May last a lifetime
For God has crossed our paths
For now
Forever

Let our quarrels be few
Our battles, measured
Let us employ patience
And understanding
Let our words be gentle and soft
Upon the ears
And upon the heart

Let the words of our Lord be our guide
So that our words and actions are born of
wisdom and kindness
And so that we may remain sisters
Kindred spirits
For all time

CHILD

For you I seek guidance
For you I pray for the best of all things
For you I beseech your guardian angel to
watch tirelessly
Without rest
So that no trouble should follow you
No harm should befall you
No evil should ever approach you

And I pray that I will be worthy to lead you
To guide and protect you
With faith and courage
With hope
With knowledge of all things that will send
you down the straight and narrow
The road to salvation
From child to man
Worthy to call himself
A Christian[⊕]

[⊕] From "Prayer in Poetry". Used By Permission.
Copyright ©2008 V. Andriotis

MOTHER

Beautiful Mother
Gentle soul
Whose child is like no other
Who selflessly and faithfully
Brought into our world
The one and only light
That can never be extinguished

With great admiration
And gratitude
With reverence
We glorify you
We pray to you

For your courage
For your strength
We praise you

For the Mother
First
Before and above all others
We stand
In awe[⊕]

A MOTHER PRAYS

That his spirit be indestructible
That he finds joy at every turn
That faith determines his direction
And that his angels protect him from harm

For this a mother prays

That his eyes see only beauty
That his heart knows only love
That he is wise beyond his years
And that his years are many

For this a mother prays

And that I stand before him, beside him, and
behind him
For years to come

For this,
A mother prays[⊕]

[⊕] From "Prayer in Poetry". Used By Permission.
Copyright ©2008 V. Andriotis

THEIR LIGHT SO SHINES

Their light so shines Oh Lord
That inspiration fills my being
Be near them that they should continue to
inspire us
And grow to serve You
That they bring joy to their mothers' hearts
Laughter to a stranger's
And glory to Your name
That their praise for You
Their love for You
Their faith in You
Are evident in the words they speak
And the actions they take

May they continue to light our way
With the love and joy that shines within
them
And with the peace and innocence that
makes us
All
Long to be children again[⊕]

[⊕] From "Prayer in Poetry". Used By Permission.
Copyright ©2008 V. Andriotis

FROM PARENT TO CHILD

I ask for the strength
To let him grow, and leave the comfort of
my embrace

I ask for the ability
To see it as the blessing that it is, for he is
growing and strong, and must begin to find
his way

I ask that You guide and protect him
When I am not near

I ask that you help him
To embrace what may seem unfamiliar, and
that he move towards it fearlessly and
eagerly

I ask that he find love and friendship
Knowledge and enlightenment

And that I may feel peace, knowing that his
guidance and protection
Comes
From above[⊕]

[⊕] From "Prayer in Poetry". Used By Permission.
Copyright ©2008 V. Andriotis

DAUGHTERS AND SONS

Our daughters and sons
Lives constructed
Around their very existence
And with much delight
And fervor
We do so

They shall inherit the earth
And Heaven
And must be prepared
Through our guidance and prayers

We must lead them from sin
And away from all things offensive to You
And they shall be called blessed
And innocent
And worthy
To inherit the earth

SLOW TO WRATH

I will not snatch the bait from your hands
For I know
That it is only presented
to lure me to anger
I do not find myself
Susceptible to such things
For I have found my peace
In the Lord
And in the words of our savior
And as my guide to all things instructs
Be "slow to wrath, for the wrath
Of man does not produce the
Righteousness of God."[⊕]

I shall, instead, be patient
And pray that you find
Peace within yourself
So that you no longer crave to tempt
Those more believing
Than you

[⊕] The Holy Bible (NKJV) – James 1:19-20

WITH YOU

Lord
The world
So full of disappointments
Lives are not always as they appear

Lead us from dark thoughts
Help us to restrain
Words spoken in haste
Without proper thought to their
consequences

Show us that we have no need
But to rely on You alone
That, with You, our actions can be
thoughtful
Our words, sensitive to each other's feelings

With You
We can feel like ourselves
We can feel truth
And
We can feel
Loved

THE LIGHT

Star streaked sky
Dripping from above
I send my prayers upward
And pray for the light to touch me
To fill me

I pray for my life to be blessed with a
healthy child
With a family untouched
By the sins of the world

I pray to be loved
Unconditionally
To be warmed
And strengthened by it
And to return it

I pray that I am reminded of it
In every face I see
And every word I say
I pray

I AM BUT ONE

For I am but one
Though the voices of many find their way
higher
From where they began
Those, sent upward
Believing
Reach their destination

I am but one
Among the voices of many
The voices of mothers
The voices of daughters
From those who care
And those who are cared for
For each other
About each other

My voice is but one
My prayers are many
I pray
Believing
That they will be heard
Even though
I am
But one

YOUR FAITH TODAY

How is your faith today?
Through war
And poverty
Mothers struggle
Children cry
It is
Exactly
Then
That your faith should be greatest
It is
Exactly
When it is most needed
Without it, you shall never see
The other side of your
Struggles, your plight
They will seem never ending
With faith, you will come through
The other side
And looking back
Be humbled
And looking up
Be grateful
And looking forward
Be glad

UNCERTAIN

Heavenly Father
Lord
Creator of all things
Only You can know
The outcome of our actions
Our decisions

Lead me to the choice
That is pleasing to You
That is Your will
What should be done

I am lost
And have searched my heart
But the answer escapes me
Or is it that I am unsure, answer enough?
Is my uncertainty the message you've sent?
Am I unwilling to hear, and accept it?

Lord
Hear my prayer
And guide me
Amen

ALRIGHT

That all will be alright
If left in Your hands
Is a reality that must
Be received
Understood
Believed

That all will be alright
If we are ever mindful
That God is at work
Within each
Circumstance
Situation
Encounter
That might present itself
Or that we might find ourselves in

Through prayer
He will enlighten us
Guide us to choices and decisions
That will
Ensure
That all will be
Alright

A Day

Oh, to share a day
With husband
And child
Basking in a hope filled moment
Lovely thoughts
Most of praise and thanks
To Him
Who grants such times to us
Such love
So many
Beautiful
Precious
Moments

Oh, to share a day
In every way
With those who bring
Joy and laughter
To my heart
Is a blessing
Indeed

TEARS

Tears
Stream
From tired eyes
My joy
Has no words
My relief
Has no other expression
My faith is fortified
My love
Is multiplied
God
Shall be magnified
By all who enter here

In this home
Faithful reside
And those who know
That He walks beside us
Have crossed the threshold
And have
Found peace
Within

MOTHER'S DREAMS

Ours are
Not simple dreams
Or aspirations
They are prayers
Those hopes we have
For our lives
Ambitions
Are all for naught
If they are not
But prayers
Waiting to be answered

Prayed with unquestionable belief that our
goals will be attained
And our dreams
Realized
But only because
They are asked of the Lord
And lead to
A life of truth
Righteousness
And God

A HEART SO BLIND

I ask forgiveness
For my ignorance
For the blindness of my heart
For an un-accepting mind
That sees with the eyes of another

Ignorance and fear
Keeps us from offering ourselves
As we should
To all of God's children

It is with great lack of understanding
Hearts so cold and unwelcoming
To all who differ from us

And so
I ask,
Can you forgive
O Lord
And make blind eyes
To see?

WITH COMPASSION

Lord
The ability
The inclination
And the strength
To see all your children
As you intended
Equal
Innocent
Only seeking love

Allow us the capacity
To love
Unconditionally
Without regard
To hateful tendencies
Of the world
But only with
Compassion and concern
For the needs
Of
Our children

Amen

BY HEART

A Mother
Becomes
A Mother
Not by nature
But
By heart
By instinct
An invisible string
Connecting her
Instantly
Effortlessly
To her child
Like no other
It is
Inexplicable
It is
Undeniable
Electric
From Heaven to Earth
Mother to Child
An unbreakable string
To each other's
Hearts

POSSIBILITIES

Oh Lord
I pray
That this house be filled with laughter
That our lives be full of possibilities
That our love be ever growing
That our family be strong
And faithful

I pray
That God is in our actions
And in our reactions

May we continue to walk through life
Together
With grace
Attaining wisdom
Maintaining our faith
And being ever closer
To each other
And to God

Amen

THE LORD PROVIDES

My arms were made
To catch you when you fall
To hold you when you cry
To rock you to sleep

The Lord provides

To you
A mother
Whose love
Can be felt in her arms
Can be seen in her eyes
Can be heard in her voice

The Lord provides

To me
A child
Whose smile
Is the light in the dark
The dream I can hold
The prayer that's been answered

The Lord
Provides

NOW

There is no time
Better than now
No moment
Will ever be quite the same
No reason
Adequate enough
To justify the absence
Of emotion
Or the open expression
Of our love
To our children
To each other

Today is the day!
Now is the moment!
Not one should pass you by
Without first expressing that love
For it takes precedence
And when it does
All else
Will follow

HERO

For a mother
For she who is nearest
To the truest sense of the word
The Lord has granted the qualities
The attributes
The gifts
Found only in those
Regarded as
Heroes

Courage
Nobility
Selflessness and love
Are her defense and response
To the needs
To the troubles
Of the world

Quiet hero
May you revel in the admiration of your
children
And may they grow to be
As you have led them
For you are blessed
And are
Their hero

Amen